**Parodies Lost**

some poems b...

What *is*

Some would say it's nothing mo... ...u mode of discourse, barely disguising a pau... ...agination and wit; a ride hitched on the coat-tails of genius, by writers or artists with no original or valuable thoughts of their own.

And if that is how you view it, you can just *SOD OFF*! 'Cos I'm a bleedin' post-modern intellectual, and I say it's all about *intertextuality*, all right?

Troubadours from John Dowland to Leonard Cohen have harnessed their inner miserable gits, taking the personal and communicating something universal, and even consoling. But, as a parodist, I can take that 'we've all been there' vibe, and make it all about *me*, as in the poem which riffs on Hardy's melancholic mopings, adding humorous touches to throw my abject misery into sharper relief.

Most of all though, it's about having a laugh, with varying degrees of reverence (or disdain) for the source material. Like Carroll with Southey, we can poke fun at a *schmaltzig* original, or use a familiar original to satirise something else altogether.

I hope the following verses will serve to demonstrate the wide variety of effects that can be achieved by ~~stealing from~~ revisiting over-familiar and even forgotten works, from updated comedy, to trivialised sincerity and even embittered social comment.

Now shut up and leave me alone.

**Self Portrait**
(after Robert Indiana)

# Discontents

# By way of introduction …

## Dai Lowe and Friends
(solo performance)

Are you doing a show? people often enquire
As I stroll down the Mile in some garish attire
Or stand at the bar like the brightest of sparks
Making ev'ryone laugh at my comic remarks.

I have gags, songs and anecdotes, some little wit,
But perform them to order? That's heavier shit.
I don't think I could, as a matter of fact,
Stand up ev'ry night and repeat the same act.

I've known any number of talented guys
Who can raise gales of laughter or gasps of surprise
In a pub or an office, far better than I —
But put us on stage and we'd probably die.

As it is, if I'm being flamboyant or loud
Just depends on my mood — or that of the crowd;
And then, if I feel I'm beginning to bore
I can shut up and let someone else have the floor.

If I choose to act flashy with tiresome persistence,
It's a way to embrace and enhance our existence.
Life IS a performance, sir, didn't you know?
Why spoil it by pausing to put on a show?

2010

## Confessional
(after Gilbert & Sullivan)


I am the very master of the intertextual reference
I use them just for fun but with a large amount of deference
My poetry is brimming with a thousand writings notable
In fact I squeeze them anywhere that I find something quotable

(In fact he puts them anywhere that he finds something quo-ta-quotable)

There's Shakespeare, Joyce and Oscar Wilde and loads of lines from G&S
And Tolstoy, Proust — well, anything that isn't just by me, I guess.
When folks say all my writing looks like something copied from a list
I simply say that I prefer to call myself 'post-modernist'

(He likes to think that he's post modern-odern-odernist)

I quite accept my writing has no true originality
But anything I do that's new just doesn't have the kwality
You're bound to fail if you don't play up to your natural aptitudes
Dan-Brownian motion only leads to loads of fuck-filled platitudes

(He has a filthy mouth and a bad atti-attitude!)

There is no end in sight (I tell you, just in case you're wondering)
I quite intend to go on with my literary plundering
As long as I can do it with due relevance and deference,
For I am the very master of the intertextual reference!


2011

## Bathetic fallacy

I have a muse perverse that spurs me on
(or would do were I not so sodding lazy).
Yesterday's intent, today is gone;
Last night's ideas, by morning far too hazy.

In all artistic fields invention thrives;
I'm filled with hope by each new inspiration,
convinced my work will touch a million lives —
but something robs me of all motivation.

My labours left unfinished would amaze.
So what's the catch? I'll tell you what the catch is —
I have a speech of fire that fain would blaze —
if only I could find the bloody matches!


2010

# Parodies Regained

## *Au Louvre*
(after Francis Thompson, *At Lords*)

It is more I am drawn to the paintings of the Northern folk,
Though Italian artists seem to steal the show;
It is more I am drawn to the paintings of the Northern folk,
Though Italian artists rule the roost, I know.
But my heart is moved more deeply by a small domestic scene
Or demons stretching bodies on some devilish machine
Or an isolated watermill beside a Flemish stream,
Where the evening swallows flicker to and fro,

To and fro ——
Oh my Ruisdael and my Breughel long ago!

2010, *au* Royal Scottish Academy

## Verses on the 65th Birthday of Peter D Lowe, Esq.
(after Lewis Carrol, after Robert Southey)

"You are old Father Peter", his family purred,
"And your bus pass is shiny and new,
"So we'd like to be certain that you're well insured,
"And your will is right up to date too."
"Though I'm sure it won't please you to hear," said their Dad,
"I can say, without any regrets,
"That I've spent far more money than I've ever had:
"So you'll only inherit my debts."

"You are old, Father Pete," said his children with mirth,
"And you've never been much of a rover,
"Yet you recently travelled half way round the earth:
"Why start now, when your youth is well over?"
"In the war," the old hero responded with glee,
"I shelled the Far East for a bet;
"So I thought it was time that I went back to see
"If they've finished repairing it yet."

"You are old, Father Pete, and we feel we must add
"That you've never been noted for taste
"But now you buy trendy new outfits like mad:
"Don't you think that's a bit of a waste?"
"Years ago," he explained, "it was never much fun
"Buying clothes which were soon out of date
"But now I'm encouraged by my eldest son
"Next to whom an old sack would look great."

"You are old Father Peter," his offspring all cried,
"And your gut keeps increasing in size
"But there's hardly a foodstuff that you haven't tried
"Do you think, at your age, this is wise?"
"In my youth," Father Peter replied with a sigh,
"Nowt exotic would get past my lips
"Now I've sampled Italian, Chinese and Thai
"But I still prefer sausage and chips."

"You are old Father Pete," said the family Lowe,
"And it's time you were settling down,
"Yet you're out on the golf course come sun, rain or snow
"And at night you go out on the town!"
"In the past, when I watched the tv from my chair,
"You complained that my sloth was a sin.
"Now I'm active, you're whinging that I'm never there —
"It would seem that I can't bloody win!"

"You are old Father Pete, if you see what we mean,
"And your hair grows increasingly grey
"Yet you chase after girls like a lad of sixteen:
"Why on earth are you acting this way?"
"In your youth," the old bugger replied to his brood,
"You showed very little respect;
"But your questions today are exceedingly rude —
"Now sod off, or I'll break all your necks!"


1990, to my Father (1925–2012)

(Carroll's *You are Old, Father William*, was itself a piss-take
  of Southey's moralising poem *The Old Man's Comforts*)

## On Hampstead Heath

(after Thomas Hardy, *At Castle Boterel*)

As I walk up the hill from the ponds for boating
  And the drizzle bedampens my threadbare shirt
I look back down through the twilight's gloating
  And see on its slope, now mired with dirt,
     Through eyes that hurt

Myself and a girlish form together
  On a drier day. We climb the lane
And reach a bench.  We sit, though whether
  For love or easing of footsore pain,
     I can't explain.

What we said as we climbed or what we were thinking
  Matters not much, nor the sex in the trees;
And whether 'twas coffee or wine we'd been drinking
  Outside Café Mozart is lost on the breeze.
    Like my mud-stained knees,

It's been scrubbed clean by time and love's forgetting,
  And all that remains is the thought it was nice
And should never have ended.  But no point in fretting
  Or letting the value be marred by the price.
    Take the wise man's advice,

And try not to weep that the good times are ended
  But smile at the knowledge that great times were had.
They might have gone sour had their days been extended:
  Just tell yourself this, and try to be glad,
    And not to go mad.

Now to me, though my love has grown bigger,
  Her heart is turned cold as a stone;
So the sun sets now on a solit'ry figure
  Who gazes, sad, at his unringing phone,
    And sits there alone.

"Hampstead Heath", as it tells us on Wikipedia,
  "Rests on a deep band of London Clay,
"Is rambling and hilly;" but none of the media
  Refers whatsoever to that long-lost day
    When we two passed that way.

But I look and see us there, fading, fading;
  I look back at it through the rain,
Not minding if folks find my tears degrading
  For I shall never be halfway sane
    Ever again.

2012

## Psychopathic Nurse

(inspired by John Cooper Clarke)

All things come to he who waits, as some thick prat once said
But before you rush in blindly where those cheering angels tread
Just pause a while and ask yourself, which option would be worse —
A psychiatric patience or a psychopathic nurse?

You never know quite where you stand, no exes mark the spot
Her heart is stone, her blood runs cold, but the rest of her is hot.
You're on a roller coaster with no brakes and no reverse —
You lose your heart, you'll lose your mind to a psychopathic nurse

Your body's on the table, your emotions on the rack;
She takes your pulse and raises it but never gives it back.
A thousand mocking Cupids pronounce the dreadful curse —
You're banged up in a padded hell with a psychopathic nurse

Oh, she can make the patient but not disturb the bed;
She treats all of your senses and discharges you half dead.
As you climb aboard the night bus, it's a double-decker hearse —
May you ever rest in pieces with your psychopathic nurse

1986

**Obelisk and Tangerine**
(after Henri Matisse, *Odalisque and Tambourine*)

# That's yer Lottery

(after Alfred, Lord Tennyson, *The Lady of Shallot*)

I dreamed last night that Sky News said
"The King is Queer, the Queen is Dead."
And then intoned the words of dread
"The country has been sold instead
To bingo callers, Camelot"
Maggie the family silver sold
Then Tony gave away the gold
The future's bright?  The future's cold.
 I'm sorry — that's yer lot.


Your last right's gone, don't call a priest
This sceptred isle has been re-leased
Tagged with the barcode of the Beast
Your one-way ticket to the feast
Sponsored by good old Camelot
So Mr Starbuck takes the wheel
While Ronald serves a Crappy Meal:
Blandness with no hope of appeal —
I'm sorry — that's yer lot.

Though oil supplies have passed their peak
Consumption rises week on week.
One wonders what on Earth the meek
When their inheritance they seek
Will get from lofty Camelot.
So one last wasteful short-haul flight
Goes mental into that good night
No use to rage at dying light
I'm sorry — that's yer lot.


While other ways I would endorse,
My pen's run dry, my throat is hoarse
My parody has run its course.
My arguments have little force
Against the might of Camelot.
And so good luck to one and all
Six numbers *and* the bonus ball
I'll see you in the shopping maul
That really is yer lot.


2006
(… when Camelot controversially won the right to continue running
the lottery, despite a tender from Richard Branson which — so he
claimed — would cream off less in profit and give more of the
proceeds to chariddies and in prizes)

### La Barista sans Merci
(after John Keats, *La Belle Dame sans Merci*)


Oh what's up with thee, sad old git,
  That you sit there faintly wittering?
Your cappuccino has gone cold
  And your phone don't ring

I see a biscuit by thy cup
 Its sell-by date proclaims it old
And on thy plate a croissant stale
  All flecked with mould

I met a lady in a caff
  Her flashing eyes my soul unlocked
Ambrosia her espressos were
  And her lattés rocked!

I spent whole days just sitting there
  Until the caffeine wrecked my heart
While she was there I found that I
  Could not depart

She made me cappuccinos sweet
  With syrups rich with flavours new
And in her accent strange she said,
  "I fency you!"

She took me to her Sighthill flat
　　And we the night in passion spent
She asked if I could spare some cash
　　To pay her rent

Right there, shagged out, I fell asleep
　　And there I dreamed, oh bugger me,
The last damn dream I ever dreamt
　　With spirit free

I saw sad poets, musicians too,
　　Each sat and nursed his gelid cup.
They cried, "*La barista sans merci*
　　Has fucked you up!"

I saw their coffees, void of foam,
　　Their mouths a hollow, silent laugh,
And I awoke and found me here
　　In this cold, drear caff

And that is why I sojourn here
　　Alone and faintly wittering
Though my cappuccino has gone cold
　　And my phone don't ring


2013,

from *Life, Measured Out: lonely visits to the coffee shops of Edinburgh*

## Constance and the Elephant

(after Marriott Edgar)

### I

It's a long way from Nott'n'm to London.
It were further in Nineteen-nineteen:
There were no motorway, so it took half a day,
And young Connie had never yet been.

Constance Lilian Priestley
Worked in the textile trade.
She were eighteen years old, rather timid than bold,
But a pretty and lively wee maid.

So when t'mill owner told 'em that summer,
They were off for a trip to the zoo,
Our lass were delighted and very excited
And probably proper chuffed too.

Remember TV weren't invented
And Attenborough (Dave) not born yet.
For a working-class child to see animals, wild:
Well, a picture book's closest you'd get.

Lions and tigers and monkeys!
(They may not mean that much to us)
But the creature that she most wanted to see
Were an elephant, big as a bus!

She just couldn't wait for the day of the trip
And her mind, I need hardly remark,
While she worked on her seams, and at night in her dreams,
Were as crowded as old Noah's Ark.

At last came the day of their outin'
She were wearin' her best summer dress
It were pretty and light (but not showy or tight)
And it cost two days' wages, no less.

We'd better say nowt of the coach trip:
Just like any school outing today;
Crackin' rather crude jokes, makin' eyes at stray blokes
And singin' daft songs all the way.

## II

At last they arrived, down at Regents Park Zoo
And to start they piled into the caff
For summat to eat: "Is this kangaroo meat?"
Connie asked, which made everyone laugh.

Lions and tigers and monkeys,
And hundreds of others besides!
Back then, at the Zoo, you could feed 'em all too
And climb up on t'big uns for rides.

But young Connie were gettin' impatient;
She said nowt, not to make any fuss;
Till her eyes, they grew wide, when at last she espied
An elephant, big as a bus!

"Are t'a goin' to feed 'im, our Connie?"
And though Connie were timid and shy,
She said that she would, 'cos she'd bought 'im some food
(Even though he seemed thirty foot high).

So Connie stared up at the creature:
At first it were all rather fun:
She curtseyed wi' charm and she 'eld out 'er arm
And showed him a large currant bun.

The elephant stared down at Connie
The elephant reached out 'is trunk
But when it came near, she got taken wi' fear
And she pulled 'er 'and back in a funk.

"Give 'im the bun, you great cissie!"
Her colleagues were havin' a ball.
"'E just wants 'is cake, and yon's 'ardly a snake —
"It's only 'is nose, after all!"

Well, strangely, that weren't reassurin' —
To be touched by a nose seemed all wrong:
A nose wrinkly and grey, that could snatch things away —
And a nose that were near four foot long!

# III

But our Connie were not to be beaten;
She'd hate to be seen as a wuss.
So, proudly, she sniffed and re-offered 'er gift
To the elephant, big as a bus.

The elephant stared down at Connie
Quite content to forgive (not forget)
And to feed 'im she tried, ee, so 'ard she near cried,
But she still couldn't do it, not yet.

As the elephant reached for the bun in 'er 'and
Connie pulled it away wi' a squeal
And 'e groaned wi' despair, as 'is trunk grabbed thin air;
All this fuss over such a small meal!

"Give 'im the bun, you great cissie!"
'Er chums all repeated wi' laughter
"'E' won't do you no harm and it isn't yer arm —
"It's only the bun what 'e's after!"

"Give 'im the bun, you great cissie!"
And so she resolved, there and then
To make one last attempt to dispel their contempt
And she 'eld out 'er 'and once again.

The elephant stared at the bun in 'er 'and
You could tell that the fellow weren't sure.
'E felt 'e'd been teased and were mighty displeased,
When young Connnie withdrew it once more.

The elephant stared down at Connie.
'E seemed to be tremblin' wi' rage
But 'e calmed 'isself down and turned slowly around
And retired to the back of 'is cage.

"Now look what tha's done: tha's upset 'im!"
Said 'er mates, as she stared at the floor.
"We didn't just come to tease animals, dumb —
"That's what our kid brothers are for!"

# IV

They weren't takin' much notice o' t'creature
'Cos they thought it were such a good game
To poke lots of fun at young Con and her bun
As t'poor lass 'ung 'er 'ead down, in shame.

They weren't takin' much notice o' t'creature
And if they were, what would they think?
That 'e'd just wandered off, stuck 'is trunk in 'is trough —
'E were obviously 'avin' a drink.

So when t'elephant walked back to t'front o' 'is cage
They thought it were really good fun
To say, "Look, it's yer friend; 'e don't want it to end:
 "'E must 'ave come back for 'is bun!"

The elephant stared down at Connie
And Connie looked up at his nose —
Which pointed straight at her and sprayed 'er wi' watter
And soaked 'er from t'noggin to t'toes!

Poor Connie just stood there all drippin'.
She cried, "Look at me best summer dress!
"It's all soaking wi' grot — and elephant snot
"I must look a complete ruddy mess!"

Her friends they were quite sympathetic
Though they couldn't 'elp laughin' a lot
And they did what they could to make 'er look good —
When they'd cleaned off the elephant snot

And Connie 'erself saw the 'umorous side:
You can't keep a young girl's spirits down.
And they say that she sang on the old charabanc
All the way back to Nottingham town

But when she got home, all bedraggled
'Er mum and dad made a right fuss
"Ee, what 'appened today?  Did it rain?" She said, "Nay:
"'Twere an elephant, big as a bus!"

2006 (a true tale of my Grandmother)

# Ticklish Allsorts

## Salmond Chanted 'Evening'

(You may not have heard, but in September 2014, people living this side of the Border have a chance to say whether they wish to remain a vassal region of the Kingdom of Bullingdon Bankers, or to rebrand themselves as the People's Republic of Salmondia. Or something like that. This is not so much about that choice, but the fact that the first casualty of a referendum campaign is truth — or, it would seem, anything remotely resembling rational debate.)


According to the Scottish *Mail*,
Yer jobs're doomed, yer crops'll fail,
Yer bairns will all end up in jail,
If youse vote 'Aye';
Yer teeth'll rot, yer pies turn stale —
And then ye'll die.

The 'Salmond' will replace the pound
(Wan hunnerd 'Sturgeons', I'll be bound);
Its value, mair dire than its sound,
Will plunge in stages,
Till just tae buy yer pals a round
Tak's three month's wages.

If Darling's pleas are a' rejected,
Mandat'ry kilts will be inspected,
And men wi' pants will be ejected
Frae this fair land.
If wily Alex gets elected,
Sex will be banned.

Och, swallow a' this propaganda,
A' this pathetic trumped-up slander,
Ye'd think this place the next Ruanda,
Wi'out a doot;
And even Embra's baby panda
Wad get kicked oot!

But don't assume yon ither lot
Are ony better, 'cos they're not;
Wi' their rose-tinted tommy-rot
An' tartan shite.
What chance has puir wee Scotty got
Tae choose aright?

So I'm no saying 'Aye' or 'Nae',
Or tryin' tae tell ye which damn way,
On thon braw, bricht September day,
Ye ought tae go;
It's no fer Sassenachs tae say,
Based here or no.

But, Ah'm a man o' Northern bent,
Whose folk them London powers resent,
And offer no encouragement,
So please tek 'eed:
Let yer new border be the Trent —
Not just the Tweed!


2013

# Philosophy Museum in Cash Crisis

*Some talk of Aristotle, of Kant and Socrates,*
*Of Bergson and Spinoza and such great names as these*


Oh, do not ask '*where is it?*' of a place what don't exist:
The Museum of Philosophy is far too eas'ly missed.
The Government won't fund 'em and they've gone into arrears
So they're forced to raise the dosh they need by selling off ideas.

They've closed the Marx and Engels wing – politic'ly unsound
And thrown out moralistic thoughts that no one wants around.
Truth and Beauty, in the Forms Room, they're fighting hard to save –
See *the Socrates Experience* from a large glass-fibre cave.

Then go out, past Good and Evil to the Friedrich Nietzsche wing
 (Ignoring nihilists who tell you it don't mean a thing)
The Berkeley Room's kept Locked unless somebody wants to see it
And Hobbes and Hume don't have a room: there's nowt it's like to be it.

The Larkin room is popular, there's a video display
Where kids can press a switch and have their parents blown away.
The Deconstruction Annexe pulls the punters in all right
But it costs so much to pay the staff to clean up ev'ry night.

The Theology curator prays for guidance from above
And the New Age people still believe that *all you need is love*
("The Oriental Rooms were such a hit in sixty eight
We're sure they'll get another life, we only have to wait")

Existentialism's doomed and there's no place for Solipsists
Who believe that just one person (who may not be them) exists.
The realists and pragmatists accept that there's no cure
When your critics are a load of Kants whose reason's far from pure

*La foratura di Veneri*
(after Edgar Degas)

In the nineties non-society we have no place for thought:
Blimey, even Roger Scruton's being hunted down for sport
(And it was his consultancy which started all this rot
With its pioneering slogan *They don't think, therefore they're not*)

And they'll respond, if you ask why admission is so dear,
"Though we agree that man's born free, it costs to come in 'ere"
And very soon the day will come when none of us can tell
The thinkers from the wankers or the heavenly from Hell

*Some talk of Aristotle, of Kant and Socrates,*
*But all the thoughts they left us are now mere commodities*

c1992

## Translation: The Girls of Llanbadarn

(or *The Last Unlaid Minstrel*)

Frustrated passion bends me double
A plague on girls, they're too much trouble!
Because I never get a lay
from any one in any way.
No sweet young thing, no cheeky bitch
No naughty wife nor ugly witch

What nastiness, what sinful traits
Make me so crap at finding mates?
Yet no fair lass e'er deems it good
To take me to some thick, dark wood.
No shame for her if there we fled
To roll upon a leafy bed

Throughout my life I always loved
(So clinging has my ardour proved:
More than the guys down Garwy way!)
One or two girls every day
Yet even so I never scored
With one I fancied — or abhorred.

In Llanbadarn no Sunday passed
(Now pious folks will be aghast)
But I'd be eying up some broad
With just my neck turned to the Lord.
And after I had long surveyed
The parish beauties, thus arrayed,
You'd hear one bright, fresh little chit
Say to her friend, who's known for wit:

"That pale lad with the sneaky face
"And girlish hair all o'er the place —
"He's got bad things on his mind
"His ways are of the evil kind!"

"So that's the nature of his lies,"
The other sexy minx replies,
"Do it with him? Ha! What a farce!
"The stupid twat can kiss my arse!"

It's rough for me but beauty's curse
Repays me with a meagre purse
No recompense my ardour wins
But sticks me with frustration's pins.

Somehow I'll have to cut this noose
If all I'm left is self-abuse
Poor wretch, I'll run from all this strife
And go and live a hermit's life
And meditate on lessons learned
From too much looking, rearward turned.

So I, whose verses folks call great
Yet shuffle off without a mate.

*Merched Llanbadarn*, by Dafydd ap Gwilym, c1350
Translated from the Welsh, 2009

## By their anoraks shall ye know them

By their anoraks shall ye know them,
By their hair and their National Health specs
And their unpleasant smell: with their mothers they dwell
And they certainly never have sex

All alone they sit with their computers
Or discuss algorithms on-line;
They are strangers to hope, human contact — and soap
But their programming skills are just fine

Yet they may be our ultimate line of defence
Against governments, crooks and the man:
When you simply can't clean spyware off your machine
There's a guy in a bedsit who can

So while 'normal' folk treat them with caution
And the cool set regard them with mirth,
You just mark my words: be nice to your nerds,
For the geek will inherit the earth

2011

## HE, CLAVDIVS

Consider the guy she leaves you for, or the chap
she takes up with later: what if he seems crap
at everything that she once praised in you, yet now
she sings those selfsame praises louder over him? How
can this be? Were he quite unlike you, you'd say, "it's shit,
"but something in her wants a change, or maybe it
"is simply true that I am not the type she really needs;
"at least, not now"; and, though your heart still bleeds,
and every thought insists it's her mistake, at least
your ego's only slightly bruised.    But feast
your eyes on this buffoon's appearance, hear the weak
attempts at wit or intellectual utterance this freak
so entertains her with. OK, Gertrude's poor husband died,
yet even he was pained beyond the grave. It's not just pride
that's hurt, but that it leaves one nagging thought: were you as fake
and posturing a nincompoop as he? Is her mistake
a rerun of the one she made before? Or can you cling
to that self-confidence she made you feel when she would sing
*your* praises to the very skies? Is it just, on your part,
jealousy? Or is she so easily impressed, her heart
can override her common sense? Can you find excuses,
reasons even, for new delusions in old abuses,
that do not cast a shadow over you, but let you flatter
yourself that you *are* Hyperion, *he* the satyr?


2010

## Love Letters (to everyone)

Your soulmate's gone and left you all alone
And smashed to smithereens your heart of glass.
Your love lies bleeding on a slab of stone;
You snap at those who tell you, "This will pass."
You're in no mood to mind your Ps and Qs:
Why bother, when you've nothing left to lose?

Before you start to turn your pain to hate
Or nurse dark thoughts involving pills or rope,
If you ever really loved your erstwhile mate
May I point out a gleaming ray of hope?
My message is as plain as A B C,
So dry your tears and listen now to me.

Love is important only 'cause you *give* it:
What can't survive rejection can't be true.
Love is life, so go and bloody *live* it,
And show in everything you say and do,
To every street in every A to Zed,
Love grows in strength, the further it gets spread.

So just hang in there, all you love-lorn swains;
Let goodwill quench the fiercest flames of hell.
The fire of loss is swamped by True Love's gains,
So join your voices with me while we tell
Of how they brought the news from X to Y,
That Love is fine and never has to die.

2012

## This Sporting Life

We call it a game, which often confuses,
As there's never a winner but plenty of losers
And everyone plays by the rules that he chooses
And acts as his own referee

The players not screaming are usually snoring
It's rarely exciting but commonly boring
And no one has any idea of the scoring
Or when they should go in for tea

It may be a sport but it's really not cricket
And few folks can stretch to the price of a ticket
It's hardly surprising that so few can stick it
So what is its lasting allure?

Ah, that is a thing that there's no way of knowing
But life has a rather strange habit of showing
To get out of this race you just have to keep going —
You're not sick but there isn't a cure

So before you complain that the strip doesn't suit you
Or wonder why no other side will  recruit you —
Just be grateful that nobody's trying to shoot you
Or using your head as the ball

And don't give a damn if the crowd never shows up
Or the critics and fans turn their communal nose up
Either way when the timekeeper finally blows up
You're gonna be left with sod all!

2013

## Red Light Blues

I was sitting at home feeling full of self-pity,
So I took a short plane ride to Amsterdam city,
To find lots of young ladies so sweet and so pretty,
    So fair both of figure and face.

They were doing their best to give me an erection
By waving bare breasts in my general direction —
But turned out to be blokes upon closer inspection —
    Something tells me I'm in the wrong place!


When down these dark alleys a young fellow goes, he
Finds many strange windows with glows that are rosy;
But, not wishing to peer in too close or seem nosey,
    How is he to know which are men?

Those give-away signs, how come I didn't spot 'em?
Those bulges they have where real ladies ain't got 'em?
But now that I've had a few stuffed up my bottom —
    Why, I think I might go there again!


2004

## Rubaiyat

Write your story on the wind;
All your former loves rescind.
Your confession proudly shout:
"Bless me Satan, I have sinned".

As they drag you from the dock,
Lose the key and seal the lock,
No defense or alibi:
"It was pure delight to shock. "

Eating *foie gras* in your cell,
Hear the tolling of the bell,
While the window bars break up
Your panoramic view of Hell.

In the isolation ward,
Where your dying hopes are stored,
Gasp your last unheeded prayer:
"Please don't let me be ignored! "

2012

*A Tapas Bar in London*
(after Eduard Manet, *A bar at the Folies-Bergère*)

## Clerihews

Edward Clerihew Bentley
Said, most unsentiment'lly,
"For famous folk a curse is
Appearing in one of my verses"


Mr Guy Ritchie
Seen without a stitch? He
Should remain fully dressed:
Films is what he does best.


The first line of a Clerihew
(I looked it up, I know it's true)
Should 'solely (or almost solely)' consist
Of the name of the person praised or dissed.


William Topaz McGonagal
Hardly ever said "Hoots mon!" at all
But he did not just sit round doing bugger all
Rather he did take it upon himself to write
                             long rambling verses in doggerel


Edward Hopper
Came a bit of a cropper
Whenever he felt pressed
To paint someone undressed

# Smalls

### Mrs Casanova's Lament

I'm not sure if I miss him
Now he's dead and gone
His last words *were*, "I love you"
But he added, "Pass it on."

### The Rime of the Ageing Gourmet

It is an ancient gourmet and he goes among the Swiss
"Show me, dear friends, what food you make I can't afford to miss?"
They started him with muesli, then fondue and raclette;
They followed up with many cakes and lots of chocolate.
He had to buy a longer belt, his trouser seams were torn;
A sadder and a wider man, he rose the morrow morn.

1998

### Xmas Card greeting.

It isnae correct (in 'political' terms)
To say 'Happy Christmas' these days
To save giein' offence (if that makes any sense)
We reword it in mealy-mouthed  ways:

 "Happy Holidays/Year End/Seasonal Time"
Sae lang as we don't *name* the season:
Just spend a' your cash on o'erpriced trash
And forget the original reason.

I'm no a believer, I freely admit,
But I'm sad to see Noël get neutered;
Oh let it be still a time o' goodwill —
And a damn guid excuse to get blootered!

2006

## Many Pancakes

"Now, what's the problem?" asked the shrink.
"Well," I replied, "my family think
"I'm crazy." "Tell me why."
"They say I'm touched and ev'ryone makes
"Fun of me, cos I like pancakes,"
I answered with a sigh.

"I hardly think that means that you
"Are mad — I'm fond of pancakes too:
"I'd even say I love 'em"
"That's great," I cried, with deep affection.
"You must call round — see my collection —
"I've got a *million* of 'em!"

2002


## Scientific Analysis
(after Dorothy Parker)

It isn't just chemicals flooding synapses
Or particles quantumly quarking;
No, love is a waveform that never collapses —
And I must be totally barking!

2011


## Fallback

If it's good enough for Clacton
Then it's good enough for me
I'll be your last resort
If you've got no one else to see

1990

## Vealanelle

Braise or grill or roast or fry,
All of us boil down to meat;
All that's born to live must die.

In a stew or in a pie,
Give yourself a tasty treat —
Braise or grill or roast or fry.

You're a veggie weirdo? Why?
Close your eyes and just repeat,
"All that's born to live must die."

Your spirit's willing? Flesh? Oh, my!
Nothing else can taste as sweet —
Braise or grill or roast or fry.

Don't heave that disapproving sigh;
No creature can the reaper cheat —
All that's born to live must die.

Still so many beasts to try;
Still your life is incomplete;
Braise or grill or roast or fry —
All that's born to live must die.

2013

# If I could sing or write music, these would be songs …

## Avoiding Clichés Like the Plague

Well some guy makes you an offer that you just cannot refuse
So you run off with my sunshine and you leave me with the blues
Now I've nothin' left to play for and ev'rything to lose   by
Avoiding clichés like the plague

You took the wind out of my sails, I can't believe my eyes
Were all of your sweet nothings just an empty pack of lies?
You say I'm full of crap but you don't seem to realise   I'm just
Avoiding clichés like the plague

    Now ev'ry hackneyed phrase seems to fit my situation
    But I can't find no words that can bring me consolation
    The only thing to do is protect my reputation:
    Best foot forward; don't be vague

So I'm swallowin' my pride, I ain't about to blow a fuse
I'm pulling out the stops and putting on my dancin' shoes
'Cause I've ev'rything to play for and nothin' left to lose   from
Avoiding clichés like the plague

2002

## I'm Settling for Falling in Love

All the people here are crazy
And if I wasn't so darn lazy
I'd go crazy too, just thinkin' of you
But I'll settle for fallin' in love

I can hear the music playin'
From the sofa where we're layin'
I'd get up and dance but I'm in a trance
Since I settled for fallin' in love

> Oh why ask me to waste energy
> On doin' loads of stuff,
> When I've recently found, with you around,
> That breathin' is more than enough

Oh my agent keeps on ringin'
But I can't be bothered singin'
I'm so satisfied, lyin' by your side
Now I've settled for fallin'
> I don't care who's callin' —
'Cos I've settled for fallin' in love


2012

## I Know He Loves Me

I know he loves me,
Even though he's not aware of it.
He can't stop thinkin' of me,
Though he tells himself he just don't care — not a bit.
I'm so sympathetic to his plight
But what's a girl to do,
Knowing that he loves me
And wishing that he knew it too?

Everythin' about me
Keeps him awake at night.
Couldn't live without me,
If only he could see the light — that's right.
Don't know how he copes with his achin' heart;
The poor guy must be livin' in hell.
I know how much he loves me;
I only wish he knew it as well.

    He needs the woman of his dreams to make him whole,
    Though they say that ignorance is bliss.
    But unrequited love is bad for the soul —
    He needs to be aware of this!

If I don't save him,
His heart will surely break.
So how can I help him
To realise his big mistake — what will it take?
He can't forget the taste of my sweet lips,
Although we've never even kissed,
But I have no doubt he'd love me,
If he only knew that I exist!

2013